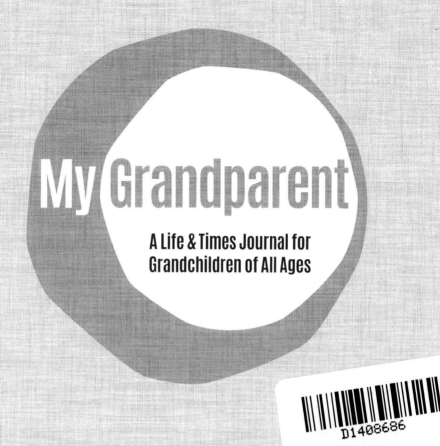

# My Grandparent

## A Life & Times Journal for Grandchildren of All Ages

Dick Edwards & Korinn S. Hawkins

ISBN: 978-0-9894003-1-2
Library of Congress Catalog Number: 2013946567

Printed in the United States of America

First Printing: August 2013

17 16 15 14 13      5 4 3 2 1

Edited by Kellie M. Hultgrean

Book design and cover design by Mary Stadelman, White Space Design

AMBER SKYE
PUBLISHING
www.AmberSkyePublishing.com
Eagan, Minnesota

To order: www.mygrandparentjournal.com or www.amazon.com

"Grandchildren are a grandparent's link to the future.
Grandparents are the child's link to the past."

*– Author Unknown*

We dedicate this book
to Pat and Corey, to our parents,
to our children and grandchildren,
and to all who support, encourage, and teach us.

# Table of Contents

# Introduction

Ask any grandparent. Ask any grandchild. At any age, the grandparent–grandchild relationship is universally celebrated as special. Grandparents are the keepers of family history and stories, of family values and culture. Grandchildren are an important link to preserving this knowledge.

*My Grandparent – A Life & Times Journal for Grandchildren of All Ages* brings grandparent and grandchild together to create a written account of the grandparent's life. It offers a series of questions that the grandchild can ask in order to write their grandparent's biography. There are also questions the grandparent can ask the grandchild to further enrich the process and the outcome.

The conversations these questions inspire will not only become an heirloom book, but will also deepen that special connection between generations. So, get ready to enjoy some valued time together and to create a book about your unique family history.

# Using This Book

*My Grandparent* provides the framework for writing a biography. It can be tailored to help the grandchild and grandparent get the most from the experience.

- Plan on several sessions to complete the process and produce the biography.

- Agree on how much time to spend during each session.

- Find a quiet, comfortable place free of distractions for talking and writing.

- The process can work as a one-on-one between grandparent and grandchild, or it can include siblings and cousins.

- Modify the use of the book to suit the grandchild's age and skill level. If the grandchild is unable to write, an adult might listen in and be the writer.

- Feel free to move around or come back to questions if you need time to think.

- There is space at the end of each chapter to add your own thoughts and questions for sharing.

- If you cannot always meet in person, consider time together using the telephone, e-mail, or video chatting.

- Take your time. Slower is better.

- End each session by setting a date for the next session.

# Enjoy!

# Title

# The Life & Times of

_____

Written by _____

_____   _____
Date Started                              Date Finished

# Family Facts

| Grandparent | Grandchild |
|---|---|
| | |
| Name | Name |
| | |
| Birth Date | Birth Date |
| | |
| Place of Birth | Place of Birth |
| | |
| Parents | Parents |
| | |
| Grandparents | Grandparents |
| | |
| Siblings | Siblings |

# Chapter **1** Growing Up Years

This chapter is about the grandparent's
childhood until leaving home to start adult life.

What do you remember about your grandparents?

What
countries were
your ancestors
from?

**What was your mother like?**

What was
your father
like?

**When and where were your parents born?**

*Where did they grow up?*

How did your
parents meet?

When and where were they married?

**What did your parents do for a living?**

_____

_____

_____

_____

_____

_____

_____

_____

_____

_____

_____

_____

_____

_____

_____

_____

_____

_____

_____

_____

_____

_____

_____

_____

_____

_____

_____

_____

_____

Tell me about
your siblings.

What were you like when you were kids?

**What activities did your family do together?**

**What three words best describe you as a kid growing up?**

*Quick Question*

Tell me about
other family members
you remember, like your
aunts and uncles
or cousins.

**What was life like in the town where you grew up?**

Tell me about
the home you
grew up in.

Tell me about your favorite room.

**What pets did you have?**

**What was your most prized possession?**

Quick Question

What
were your
hobbies?

Flip
Flib

What are
your hobbies?

**What were some of your favorite things to do growing up?**

**Flip Flib Grandparent Asks**

**What are some of your favorite things to do?**

Share a favorite memory of your growing up years.

Tell me about
your best friend
growing up.

Why did you get along so well?

Flip
Flip

Grandparent Asks

Who is your
best friend?

Why do you get along so well?

Tell me about a memorable birthday you celebrated.

**How did your family celebrate holidays?**

**Which was your favorite?**

What other family
traditions do you
remember?

**Did your family take trips or vacations?**

**Which was your favorite?**

What kind
of student
were you?

What school activities did you enjoy?

Grandparent Asks

Flip

What school
activities do/did
you enjoy?

**What was it like being a teenager when you were growing up?**

_____

_____

_____

_____

_____

_____

_____

_____

_____

_____

_____

_____

_____

_____

_____

_____

_____

_____

_____

**How did you learn to drive a car?**

**What was your first car like?**

_____

_____

_____

_____

_____

_____

_____

_____

**What was your first paid job?**

**What did you learn from working the job?**

**What historical event do you remember from when you were growing up?**

**Who was an influential person in your life growing up?**

*How did they influence you?*

What values
did you learn
growing up in
your family?

# Chapter **2** Work Life & Family Years

This chapter is about the grandparent's
work life and their years raising a family.

Tell about when you first left home to live on your own.

Where did you go?

What was it like?

_____

_____

_____

_____

_____

_____

_____

_____

_____

_____

_____

_____

_____

_____

_____

_____

_____

_____

_____

_____

_____

_____

_____

_____

_____

_____

_____

_____

_____

_____

_____

_____

Tell me about jobs
you worked as an
adult and what you
liked about them.

Grandparent Asks

Flip
Flib

What is your
dream job?

How did you
get into your
life's work?

Who was the
first president
you voted for?

Quick Question

What hobbies or community activities were you involved in as an adult?

**How did you meet my grandma/grandpa?**

**What attracted you to each other?**

_____

_____

_____

_____

_____

_____

_____

_____

_____

_____

_____

_____

_____

_____

_____

_____

**What was it like dating?**

_____

_____

_____

_____

_____

_____

_____

_____

_____

_____

_____

_____

**What do you remember about your wedding day?**

**Quick Question**

**Who were the attendants at your wedding?**

**What were your hopes and dreams for the future?**

What was it
like having your
first child?

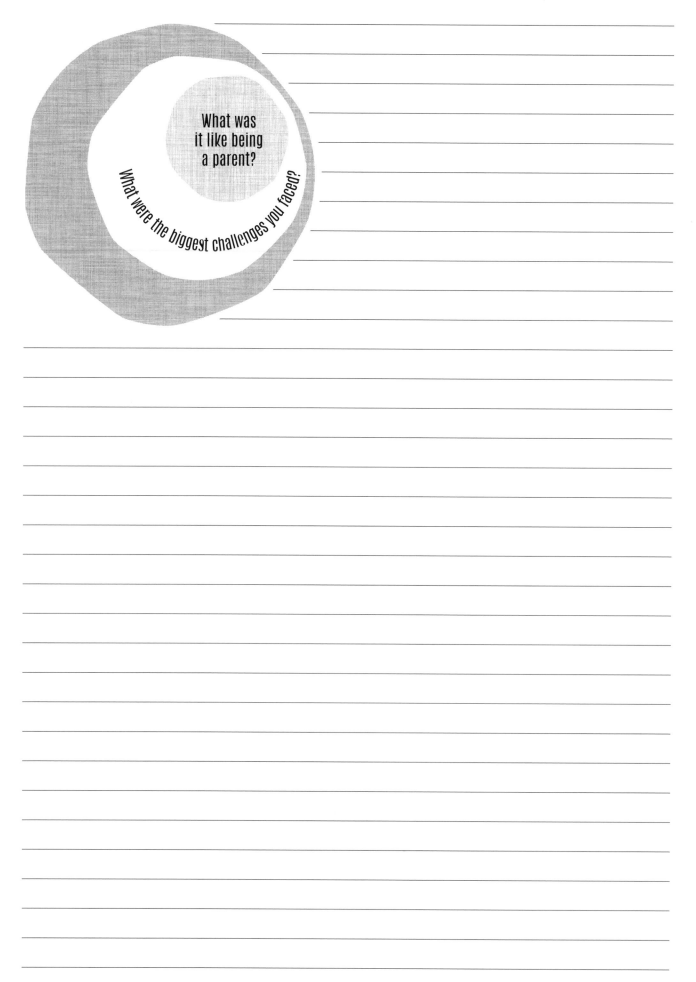

**What was it like being a parent?**

**What were the biggest challenges you faced?**

What was my mom/dad like as a kid?

Share a memory of her/him growing up.

What was something they did that made you proud?

**What kinds of things did you do together as a family?**

Did your family take any fun trips or vacations?

Which was your favorite?

**What were holidays like when your kids were growing up?**

Tell me about
the hopes and
dreams you had
for your kids.

What values did you feel were important to teach your kids?

**Flip**

What values
do you think are
important for kids
to learn?

Additional Thoughts & Questions for Sharing

# Chapter ❸ Grandparenting & Retirement

This chapter is about being a grandparent
and life after the work years.

**Tell me about when you first learned you were going to be a grandparent.**

_____
_____
_____
_____
_____
_____
_____
_____
_____
_____
_____
_____
_____
_____
_____
_____

**What was it like when I was born and you met me for the first time?**

_____
_____
_____
_____
_____
_____
_____
_____
_____
_____

Share a memory you have from when I was little.

Flip Flib

Grandparent Asks

Share a memory you have from when you were little.

**What are some of your favorite things we do together?**

_____

_____

_____

_____

_____

_____

_____

_____

_____

_____

_____

_____

_____

_____

_____

_____

_____

_____

**List 3 things that have made you proud of me.**

*Quick Question*

_____

_____

_____

_____

_____

_____

_____

_____

_____

_____

_____

_____

_____

What is the best part of being a grandparent?

**What do you wish most for your grandchildren?**

_____

_____

_____

_____

_____

_____

_____

_____

**What special things do you want our family to pass down as heirlooms?**

**Quick Question**

_____

_____

_____

_____

_____

_____

_____

_____

_____

_____

_____

_____

_____

_____

_____

_____

_____

What advice
do you want to
pass on to me?

Grandparent Asks

Flip
Flip

What special
thing do you want
your family to pass
down as an heirloom?

**When did you retire?**

**From what job?**

_____
_____
_____
_____
_____
_____
_____
_____
_____
_____
_____
_____
_____
_____
_____
_____
_____
_____

**How did you make the decision to retire?**

_____
_____
_____
_____
_____
_____
_____
_____
_____
_____
_____
_____
_____

What were you
looking forward
to in retirement?

How do you like to spend your time in retirement?

How is retirement
more or less fun
than you expected?

Why?

Additional Thoughts & Questions for Sharing

# Chapter ④ Looking Back • Looking Ahead

This chapter is for the grandparent's reflection
on things learned and on hopes for the future.

**What were some memorable historical events that occurred in your lifetime?**

**What famous person would you like to meet?**

Quick Question

What in your life
has most influenced
who you are today?

If you could start a
new family tradition,
what would it be?

Why?

_____
_____
_____
_____
_____
_____
_____
_____
_____
_____
_____
_____
_____
_____
_____
_____
_____
_____
_____
_____
_____
_____
_____
_____
_____
_____
_____
_____

What are the
most important
relationships
in your life?

**What is the best advice you ever received?**

*Who gave it to you?*

Tell me about a challenging time in your life and how you got through it.

**What are
you most
grateful for?**

**Flip
Flip**
*Grandparent Asks*

What are you
most grateful for?

What would you say are your greatest accomplishments?

**Tell me about your spiritual beliefs or church life.**

What is
something you
would still like
to do if you have
the chance?

Flip
Flip

What is something
you would like to do
if you have the chance?

What are your
hopes and dreams
for your future?

For our family's future?

Additional Thoughts & Questions for Sharing

# A Letter to My Grandparent

Write a thank-you note to your grandparent and tell what writing in this book together has meant to you.

_____

_____

_____

_____

_____

_____

_____

_____

_____

_____

_____

_____

_____

_____

_____

_____

_____

_____

_____

_____

_____

_____

_____

_____

_____

_____

_____

Write a thank-you note to your grandchild and tell what writing in this book together has meant to you.

# A Letter from My Grandparent

# Family Recipes & Photographs

Record your favorite family recipes and add some of your favorite family photographs.

Record your favorite family recipes and add
some of your favorite family photographs.

# Family Recipes & Photographs

# Family Recipes & Photographs

Record your favorite family recipes and add some of your favorite family photographs.

_____

_____

_____

_____

_____

_____

_____

_____

_____

_____

_____

_____

_____

_____

_____

_____

_____

_____

_____

_____

_____

_____

_____

_____

_____

_____

_____

Record your favorite family recipes and add
some of your favorite family photographs.

# Family Recipes & Photographs

# About the Authors

## Dick Edwards

Dick Edwards is a retired Mayo Clinic Eldercare Specialist with thirty-five years of experience in working with older adults and their families. He is author of the highly acclaimed book *Mom, Dad...Can We Talk? Insight and Perspectives to Help Us Do What's Best for Our Aging Parents.* Dick knows firsthand the lasting value of strengthening the unique grandparent–grandchild bond and capturing life stories and lessons that can only come from a grandparent.

Dick and his wife, Pat, live at their lake home in west-central Wisconsin, where they dote on six totally awesome grandchildren.

## Korinn S. Hawkins

Korinn S. Hawkins is the author and illustrator of several children's books, including *Someone Above You Loves You; Thanks God, I Love You, and Goodnight; Oh Eggs!;* and *Our Home, The Earth.* She also writes for adults and is the founder of the blog *Shine Mine.* Korinn has over ten years of experience working professionally with children and appreciates the positive impact strong family bonds can have on their healthy growth and development.

Korinn and her husband, Corey, live a busy family life with their two young and active children in west-central Wisconsin.

To learn more about Dick and Korinn, their values, and their work, go to **www.mygrandparentjournal.com**